DOWN TO EARTH

DOWN TO

EARTH

*Garden
Secrets!
Garden
Stories!
Garden
Projects
You
Can
Do!*

CREATED BY

MICHAEL J. ROSEN

and 41 Children's Book Authors
and Illustrators

HARCOURT BRACE & COMPANY

San Diego   New York   London

Library of Congress Cataloging-in-Publication Data
Down to earth/edited by Michael J. Rosen.
p.   cm.
Summary: Forty-one authors and illustrators of books
for children share their gardening experiences. Includes
various activities and recipes related to gardening.
ISBN 0-15-201341-5
1. Gardening—United States—Anecdotes—Juvenile literature.
2. Illustrators—United States—Anecdotes—Juvenile
literature.   3. Gardening—Juvenile literature.
4. Handicraft—Juvenile literature.   5. Cookery—Juvenile
literature.   [1. Gardening—Miscellanea.]
I. Rosen, Michael J., 1954–
SB457.D68   1998
635—dc21   97-11658

The display type was set in OptiPackard Bold.
The text type was set in Esprit.
Color separations by Bright Arts, Ltd., Hong Kong
Printed and bound by South China Printing Company, Ltd.,
Hong Kong
This book was printed on totally chlorine-free
Nymolla Matte Art paper.
Production supervision by Stanley Redfern
Designed by Linda Lockowitz

First edition
F E D C B A

Printed in Hong Kong

Title page illustration: Mark English

TABLE OF CONTENTS

A GARDEN'S PLOT IS MORE than just a piece of land. It's a story. Each plant is a character (some welcome, some intruders), and every season begins a new chapter, packed with births and deaths, surprises and disappointments.

Down to Earth has a most unusual plot, since everything that grows within its borders—daisy, foxglove, milkweed, pear—has been transplanted from someone else's garden. In the fertile space of these pages, autumn corn is harvested as spring primroses are gathered; asparagus springs up while watermelons fatten.

The forty-one artists and authors in *Down to Earth* have each picked a favorite fruit or vegetable—or even a weed—and shared their fascination with that plant in words and pictures. All the participants here possess a green thumb, and they all have green hearts, too. Their generosity in donating their work helps Share Our Strength send this book's profits all over the United States to community gardens, where people who are hungry can grow their own fresh produce to market or to eat. (Read more about this on pages 62–63.)

As you dig into this lovingly tended plot, I hope you'll find all the plants you love to grow, and that you'll meet a few others for the first time. That's the real story behind *Down to Earth:* a plot that grows and grows—a plot that feeds and nurtures all of us.

Michael J. Rosen

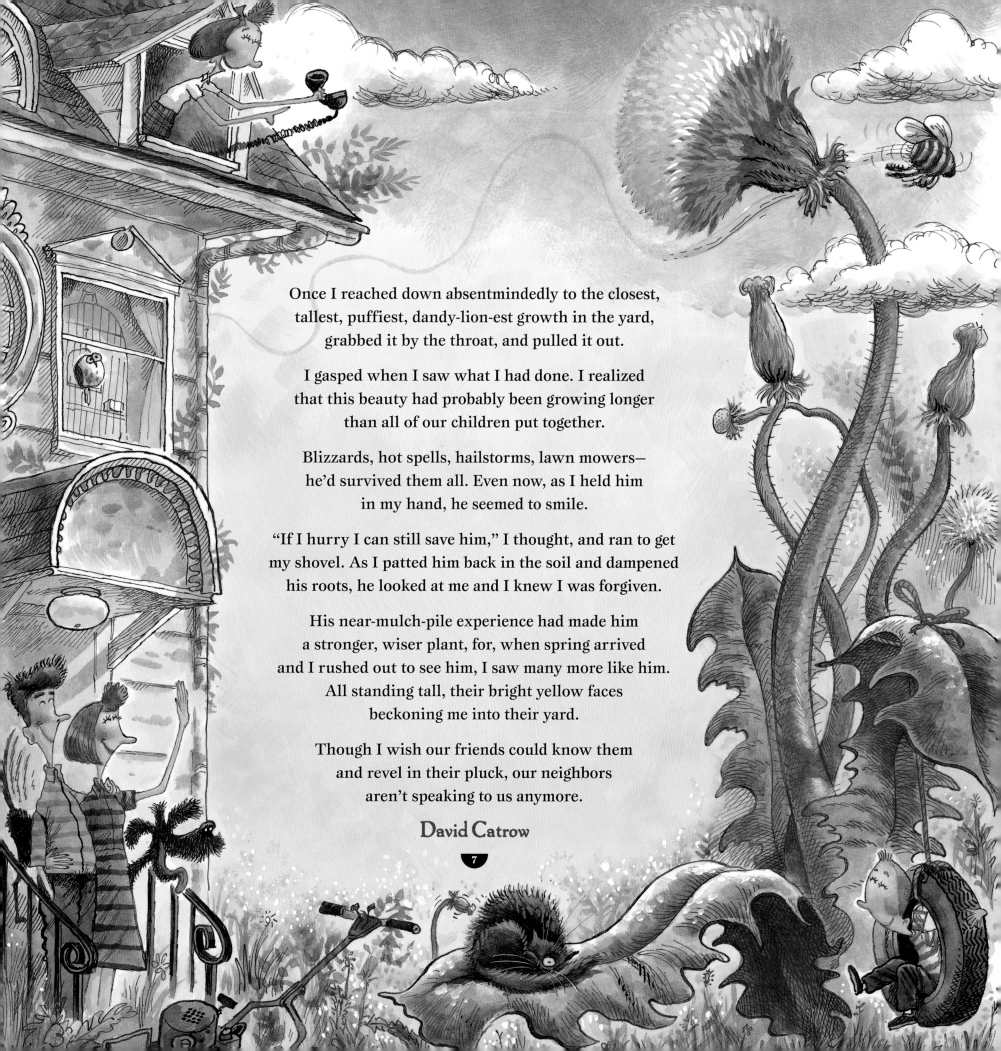

Once I reached down absentmindedly to the closest,
tallest, puffiest, dandy-lion-est growth in the yard,
grabbed it by the throat, and pulled it out.

I gasped when I saw what I had done. I realized
that this beauty had probably been growing longer
than all of our children put together.

Blizzards, hot spells, hailstorms, lawn mowers—
he'd survived them all. Even now, as I held him
in my hand, he seemed to smile.

"If I hurry I can still save him," I thought, and ran to get
my shovel. As I patted him back in the soil and dampened
his roots, he looked at me and I knew I was forgiven.

His near-mulch-pile experience had made him
a stronger, wiser plant, for, when spring arrived
and I rushed out to see him, I saw many more like him.
All standing tall, their bright yellow faces
beckoning me into their yard.

Though I wish our friends could know them
and revel in their pluck, our neighbors
aren't speaking to us anymore.

David Catrow

There is an old apple tree in the garden of the house where I was born. As a baby I gazed into its flickering leaves from my pram. As a toddler I collected its bitter little windfalls in a basket. As a child I escaped into its branches with a book and hid for hours. Seasons were measured by its snowy white blossoms in spring and the green apples swelling throughout the summer to be picked on a golden afternoon in September. The resulting apple pies and crumbles fed us well into the winter, when the tree's gnarled branches were breathtakingly beautiful in snow and frost.

And now my babies kick and crow and try to catch the blossoms, and my children swing on the branches and disappear into the rustling leaves, and savor the smell of apple crumble while I'm cooking in the kitchen. And life goes on. . . .

Jane Ray

Mom planted some ivy in the earth next to our house. Over time it crept up the walls and became home to all sorts of mysterious creatures. I helped keep the ivy trimmed so that it would grow up the wall the way that Mom had planned. If only, instead of clippers, I'd had a machine that could shrink me down to one inch tall. I'd have climbed into the leaves and had...well, who knows what kind of adventures there with who knows what kind of cool, crazy pals!

Adam McCauley

When I was nine, I lived in Ireland and went to boarding school. I went home for vacations on the train. The train was creaky and slow and stopped at every little town. In spring the banks that bordered the tracks were covered with pale yellow primroses. At each stop I'd jump off, climb the mossy, squishy bank, and nip off some flowers. Their stems were thin and as wiggly as rubber. By the time I got home, I had a bouquet for my mother. Spring stars, she called them.

It was always a scramble to get back on board as soon as the whistle blew and before the train began its slow chug onward.

One day all the best primroses were at the top of the slope. The ground was boggy and I sank in over my shoes and ankle socks. I hurried, but the whistle blew and the train left without me.

I knew all the stationmasters. This one called my mother. When she came I had fistfuls of primroses. She hugged me and said she'd never seen spring stars so beautiful.

Now I have clumps of them in my California garden. Some people say they have no perfume. But of course they do. They smell of homecoming, of mossy banks and thick brown mud.

They smell of Ireland.

Eve Bunting

My dog Daisy was the first to show me the sticks. They floated to her in shallow water along the river near our home in Montana. Each had been cut from willow trees by beavers who lived upstream. Some were long; others were six or ten inches, just right for Daisy to carry in her mouth.

For a long time I would take them from her and throw them. She likes to fetch sticks.

But, after a while, I noticed some of the thin red sticks were still covered with fresh bark. Some even sprouted strong white roots from near the thickest end.

So I took some of the sticks home. I put them in a jar and the little roots grew longer. When I took the sticks from the jar and placed them gently in soft soil near a pond, they sprouted leaves. Since the pond had no trees growing along its edges, and no beavers, I decided to plant more of the beavers' willows.

I started cutting branches myself, too, creating willow gardens in places I hoped beavers might someday come to tend them.

But beavers aren't the only ones to live with willows. I've planted my cuttings along other ponds, small streams, and big rivers where warblers nest in the willows, deer hide in their shade, and moose nibble the tender new shoots.

Not long ago I took some willows to Ohio and planted them with first graders at a place they call Moose Marsh. They hope the willows will call to the moose, bringing them all the way to Ohio from Montana. Perhaps they will come, following the paths of the Missouri, Mississippi, and Ohio Rivers.

And all this begins with a dog who can fetch sticks.

Ron Hirschi

The mushrooms come out in the spring. My brother and I race through the woods, seeking the pale caps that rise from a blanket of last year's leaves. "I saw them first," I shout. Then I snap their slender stems, drop a fistful into my sack, and run to look for more.

Back at home Grandma fries the morels in butter. With only a pinch of salt, they taste like heaven—even though they've come straight from the earth. Everybody, even my brother, gets a share.

Daniel Kirk

12

Trusted with a sharp knife, I walk slowly to the back of the yard, knife point down. Small green shoots push out of the early summer dirt. Cutting close to the ground, I fill my hands with enough tender stalks for dinner. In the late afternoon heat, I take time to share my fresh asparagus with a six-legged friend.

Julia Gorton

13

The first time
I tasted a tomato fresh from the vine,
I wanted to grow my own tomatoes. The ones from
the supermarket—plucked green and truck ripened—were
pale imitations. And so, in search of the perfect tomato,
I moved from the city to the foothills of Idaho.

Guided by organic gardening magazines, I planted
lettuce in the shade, tomatoes in the sun, and
marigolds beside the tomatoes. Marigolds,
they said, would keep nematodes from my
tomato plants. I'd never heard of nematodes—were they
related to tree frogs?—but I dutifully planted marigolds
with my tomatoes and I never even saw a nematode. The
marigolds brightened my garden with their round red,
gold, orange, and yellow heads, while the tomatoes grew
tall, their deep-green vines laden with fat red fruit. I feasted
on juicy ripe tomatoes all summer, while the tomatoes and
marigolds became colorful, inseparable companions.

In the fall, after the last tomatoes were harvested, the
marigolds remained, dropping long black-and-white-
striped seeds to help the tomatoes that would be
planted the following year. It had been a good,
long growing season, but the September frosts
were on their way, and the growing season
was definitely over. I looked forward to the
following spring, when the tomatoes and marigolds
and I would be together again.

Carole King

14

Pansies are nice with their kitty cat faces,
and I had an aunt who just loved roses—
"GORGEOUS!" she would exclaim, and her
mouth, bright with lipstick, would make
a rosy O shape just saying the word.
But me, I'm a moss kind of person.

And if moss were a person, especially a
child, it might be considered difficult, or at
least shy, for it grows within the secrets and
shadows of the earth. In forests it climbs the
north side of trees. It creeps over rotting logs
and carpets rough rocks. It despises the sun
and loves damp and dark places. I once knew
a ruined old house, and devil's grass grew
between the floorboards and moss crept up
the walls like green embroidery. I thought
they were the most beautiful walls I had ever
seen and vowed that when I grew up and
owned my own house, I would have a living
room with green walls like moss.

And I do.

Kathryn Lasky

15

Milkweed grows in places where it is not always wanted, and it spreads all over, out of control. The milkweed plants fill my back meadow, and I can keep an eye on them from my window. During summer they grow taller and bigger, their purple flowers signaling butterflies to land, their big leaves curling, and their seedpods appearing when their flowers are gone. In the fall those funny pods burst open, sending clouds of fluffy seeds into the wind—every one like a wish someone might make.

Michael McCurdy

She loves me. She loves me not.
She loves me. She loves me not.
She loves me....
It took every blossom from my
neighbor's daisy plant to arrive
at the right answer. Now in my
hand was all the evidence
I needed: *She loves me.*

With a wellspring of love in my heart,
I marched to her front door and rang
the bell. The door opened. I held up
the daisyless bouquet and proclaimed,
"YOU LOVE ME!" However, much to my
dismay, little Jane hadn't answered the
door. It was her grandmother instead.

Will Hillenbrand

Here's what you start with: a two-story fig tree, a great-grandmother named Fanny, one hot hot summer day. And singing, lots of singing. Then you take all the aluminum pie pans, the garlands, the bells (big, little, tinkly, chiming), the empty Campbell's condensed soup cans without their wrappers, the pinwheels all red and blue and yellow, and anything that's noisy or shiny or spinning or ringing, anything, *anything,* you can find, and hang it all on the boughs of the tree with its large fuzzy leaves and its not-yet-ripe fuzzy fruit. And you sing as loud as you can, all the songs you know. Dance, too.

"All this commotion down here will keep the birds away for sure," Fanny says, as she wraps the garland around the lower branches. You look up and see those birds—blue jays, grackles, a pigeon—watching from the telephone line. Rascally birds. Noisy birds. Hungry birds. But you only decorate the bottom story of the tree.

"Because those birds need some figs, too!" Fanny says.

You look at the bright green fruit that's going to turn dark, luscious brown in just a few days. The tree is full full full of figs, all the way to the top. Each limb is loaded down with figs for jelly, figs for jam, figs for pudding, figs that'll burst in your mouth the minute you pop them in.

You can't wait. The birds can't, either! You do a figgy dance right there with your great-grandmother Fanny. Figs for you. Figs for Fanny. Figs for everyone.

Kathi Appelt

You could call it a home or a cottage. Some would call it a shack. But they don't know the magic of the little house in the field surrounded by scuppernong vines. The vines were all you could see from the road, and that was fine with the families that lived there. The vines had been there longer than anything in the field and had welcomed everyone who had ever lived in the little tin-roofed house. All the families loved it there and stayed till their children grew up and left them. The vines stayed on.

When the scuppernongs were ready, everyone in that little house would stop what they'd been doing and take the day off to pick the green plum-flavored fruit from the vines. The picking was hard. Everyone worked and sweated in the sun, swigging cool water from the glass jug that was passed around. The little kids let the older ones hold the jug for them because it was too heavy. Baskets overflowed with beautiful fruit.

The pickers imagined how the scuppernongs would look in jars on the kitchen shelf. They'd watch the man from the big farm up the road press the scuppernongs to juice and perform the magic that made the bottles glimmer with Alabama sunshine.

When the time had passed for the scuppernongs, the people had taken what they needed and the birds had the rest.

Angela Johnson

19

I do not plant my garden,
but every year it appears.
On summer days I go out hunting
for those ripe wild raspberries
that glow so red against the leafy green
along the forest's edge. And then I watch as
catbirds! thrushes! bluebirds!
gobble berries, too.
On summer days I go out
hunting the tart and sweet blueberries
that lie hidden under clusters of leaves
down low, or high, in trees. And then I watch
as cedar waxwings eat the ones I've left.
This garden is for all of us—
for me and for the birds,
for all the hunters and the gatherers,
for the turtles, the chipmunks, and the slugs,
for the bees, the butterflies,
and the bugs.

Lynne Cherry

20

A potato plant grew out of a big blue Ball jar on a windowsill in my grandma's kitchen.
Its roots waved through blue water, and sunlight painted each leaf. I closed my eyes
and I was in that cool green plant world, reaching for the light.

Summer sun shimmered through panes and danced over walls, ceiling, and potato vine
in watery rainbows. As the day cooled, Grandma threw open the doors, and the
twiny, tangled potato vine, suspended in water, could rejoin the sweet peas, violets, and carnations
that dug their roots into the garden soil, with picket fence, sea wind, and sand dunes beyond.

Now every vase I fill with flowers, every potato I carve and stamp
into paintings like this one, reminds me of my grandmother and her Ball jar.

Diana Pomeroy

We sit down on a hot summer night to a huge bowl of fresh sweet corn. The whole family is slathering butter and salt on ear after ear. Everybody crunches up and down the rows of kernels. Did you know there can be up to twelve rows on a cob and up to thirty seeds per row?

Let's explore the cornfield these ears came from. Let's walk in deep, weaving our way between rows, letting the broad leaves of the plants brush against our long sleeves. The cornstalks are thick as your arm and the tassels wave like hundreds of flags high overhead. It's shady and silent, our private forest. The wind, moving through the tops of the stalks, makes the sighing sound of the ocean lapping the shore. Far off, we can hear red-winged blackbirds and crows having an argument, and if we stay very still for a long time, we might catch the little skittery noise a mother mouse makes hurrying along her pathway to the nest.

It will be August before we have full ears ready to eat. We recycle everything about the corn plant. The horses are eager to eat the outer layers of husks—we call these the shucks. The cobs themselves go into the compost pile, as they are too woody for feed. But the stalks—the stalks are like candy and the horses eat up every inch. Best of all, though, we get the corn on the cob.

Maxine Kumin

22

When I bought my mountain cabin, the old woman told me to look for tiger lilies in the summer. And one July morning, in the shade of the oaks, cedars, and pines, I saw your roaring fire! I remembered the poem about a tiger by William Blake and thought to myself: *Tiger lily burning bright, in the forests of the night…*

Each year, tiger lily, your blazing visit leaves memories. Drawing close to find the tiger, my children once saw eye to eye with you. My sister held you in her wedding bouquet. When the old woman died, I took your black-flecked flames to the library, a beloved meeting place in the village. Before anyone looked at a book, they gazed at you. Whether in the cool quiet of the library or forest, your orange beauty surprises.

Tigers and lilies, wildness and delicacy, belong together.

Malka Drucker

I've lived in apartments all my life and I love them. Living high above the ground, I can look out over everything. For years I lived alone, a carefree bachelor in sparsely furnished rooms—with no dogs, no cats, no fish, and no plants. Well, that's not exactly true; someone once gave me a cactus, but I killed it by forgetting to water it.

It's odd that I eventually married someone who loves gardening and nurturing sickly little plants that people give her until they blossom and flourish. Sometimes I'm truly amazed at the care she lavishes on her row of herbs on our windowsill and how she tends to each individual plant.

Lately, every once in a while, I find myself checking on the thyme and the basil and the . . . Just to make sure they have enough water and they're all right. And maybe, just maybe, one day we'll raise our own little seedlings together.

Dan Yaccarino

GAD ZUKES! No matter how many times I check the zucchini patch, looking for five- to eight-inch-long zucchini ready for harvesting, there is always at least one zuke that gets away—one zucchini that is the size of an inflated ball bat when I finally discover it. Zucchini squash seem to grow at night, while I am sleeping. So I figure I can either sit up all night with my flashlight trained on the zucchini patch, hoping to catch the squash before they reach gargantuan proportions, or I can pull out the "Zucchini File"—hundreds of ways to cook monster zucchini. There are recipes for steamed zucchini, fried zucchini, grilled zucchini, battered zucchini, baked zucchini, sautéed zucchini, stuffed zucchini, zucchini bread, zucchini muffins, zucchini cake, zucchini pie, zucchini pickles, zucchini jam . . .

Are you free for dinner?

Denise Fleming

As a child of the Puerto Rican diaspora, all of my life I had heard about how nature had lavished the island of Borinquén with incredible beauty. "La Isla del Encanto." My parents wistfully recollected blue skies, native flowers, and green palm trees. Now for the first time I was being driven up a winding road by my relatives who lived in the highlands of Puerto Rico, where I would be spending my summer vacation.

That was when I first saw the flamboyant trees in full bloom with their blazing red blossoms. Whenever the sun shone directly on the trees, the flowers sparkled like flames of red fire dancing upon their branches. I gasped, amazed. The radiant trees kept reappearing along the steep, narrow route that took us farther up into the mountains. I insisted that we stop the car. I wanted to touch the blossoms and see if they were really on fire. My relatives laughed at their silly New York City visitor. When I stepped out of the car, I found myself beneath a canopy of branches with delicate fernlike green leaves. I scooped up one of the many bright red blossoms that covered the ground. I saw that small petals, each about the size of a large button, attached to the stem and created an abundant flower. The blossom had no distinctive scent, yet I detected a subtle fragrance, a combination of all the aromas of this glorious forest.

That day I began to understand how the memory of these magnificent trees sustained my parents and kinfolk all those many years when they were forced to live far away from the warmth and the beauty of their cherished island of Borinquén.

Nicholasa Mohr

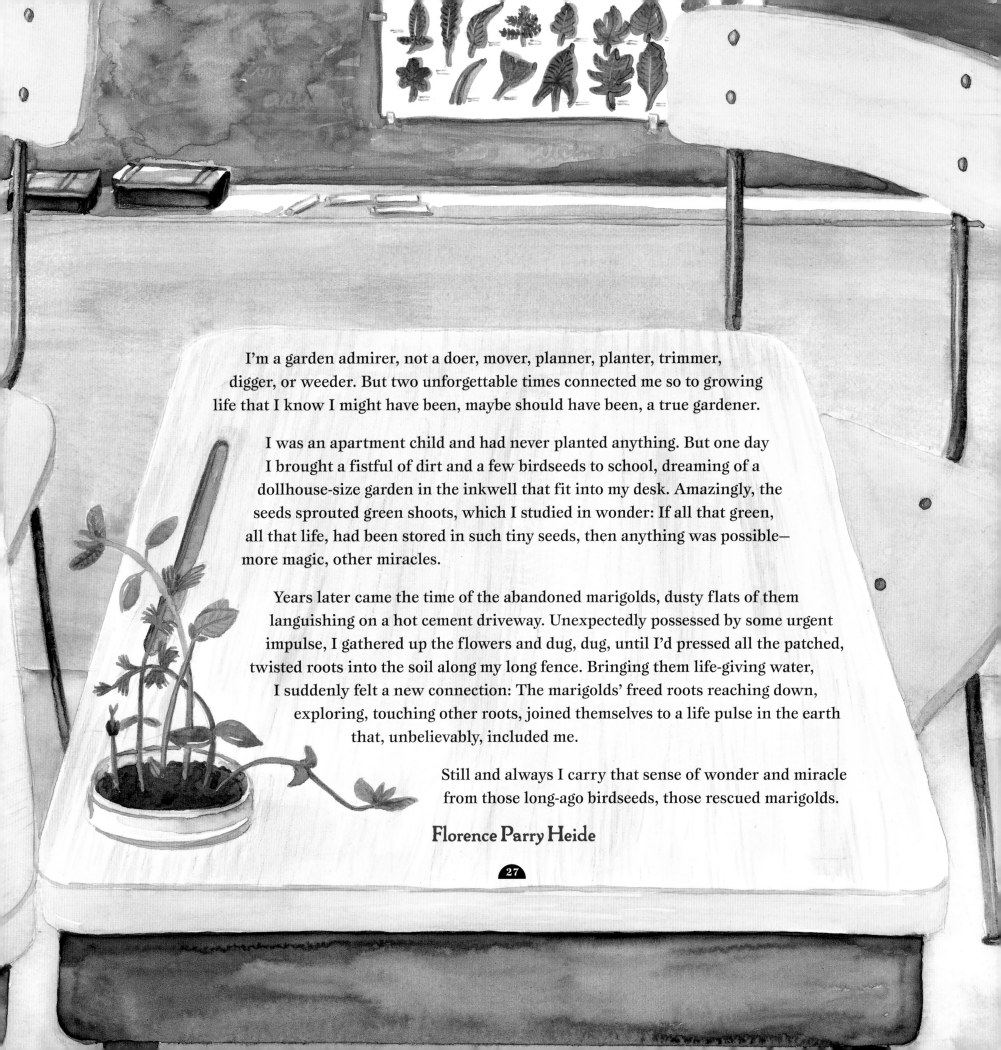

I'm a garden admirer, not a doer, mover, planner, planter, trimmer, digger, or weeder. But two unforgettable times connected me so to growing life that I know I might have been, maybe should have been, a true gardener.

I was an apartment child and had never planted anything. But one day I brought a fistful of dirt and a few birdseeds to school, dreaming of a dollhouse-size garden in the inkwell that fit into my desk. Amazingly, the seeds sprouted green shoots, which I studied in wonder: If all that green, all that life, had been stored in such tiny seeds, then anything was possible— more magic, other miracles.

Years later came the time of the abandoned marigolds, dusty flats of them languishing on a hot cement driveway. Unexpectedly possessed by some urgent impulse, I gathered up the flowers and dug, dug, until I'd pressed all the patched, twisted roots into the soil along my long fence. Bringing them life-giving water, I suddenly felt a new connection: The marigolds' freed roots reaching down, exploring, touching other roots, joined themselves to a life pulse in the earth that, unbelievably, included me.

Still and always I carry that sense of wonder and miracle from those long-ago birdseeds, those rescued marigolds.

Florence Parry Heide

27

On warm summer mornings I would wake to the smell of newly cut grass.
Back then I lived in the suburbs and someone was always cutting the lawn. My dog and I
would walk through the sleeping house, taking a pillow for me, a ball for him, and some food for us both.
We would slip out into the garden to lie on the grass and watch as the neighborhood woke up around us.

Vivienne Flesher

My wonderful mom was not a wonderful cook. Squash, I think, was on her double-dull dinner-dish list. Whether the squash was Hubbard, pattypan, buttercup, or zucchini, Mom did not bring much imagination to its preparation. Acorn squash alone defeated my mom's ability to make it unappetizing. Maybe this explains my great fondness for acorn squash. *Curcurbita pepo.*

Reynold Ruffins

Six reasons I like mustard greens:

1. Mustard greens grow from the tiniest seeds imaginable. Some kinds of mustard have ten thousand seeds to the ounce.

2. Mustard is in the Bible. Jesus told his followers that their faith should be like mustard, which is the "smallest of all seeds, but when it has grown, it is the greatest of shrubs and becomes a tree, so that the birds of the air come and make nests in its branches." (No birds have nested in my mustard yet, but they are welcome.)

3. Mustard is packed full of vitamins. If Popeye had eaten mustard instead of spinach, his name might have been Hercules.

4. Mustard is slightly bitter. I like it that way because it's the one vegetable I don't have to fight the slugs for.

5. In the spring each mustard plant bolts, sprouting a stalk four or five feet tall. On the stalk grow tiny yellow flowers, then seeds— the seeds used to make the hot-dog kind of mustard.

6. An ounce or two of mustard seeds on your doorstep is supposed to ward off witches. If a witch comes in the night, she spies the mustard seeds and is overcome by the urge to count them. This takes the witch so long that the sun rises and she has to go home.

Judy Sierra

When I was a child, we spent each summer in a cabin by a lake, deep in the Catskill Mountains, where, on hot and muggy days, thunderstorms rolled in frequently and sometimes unexpectedly. Ferns grew everywhere there, edging the woods like a lace border, filling the spaces between trees like friendly waving fans. On the other side of these woods was Miss Tray's house. We knew about Miss Tray: She was a witch! Of course, none of us ever actually saw her. We just liked having our own homespun goblin to scare ourselves with.

Some of us liked to play a game. We ran from the woods to as close to Miss Tray's as we dared to go. Whoever got the closest won. But what if Miss Tray decided to pop out and grab you? One hot and muggy day, my friend Susie and I stood at the edge of the woods. The sky was darkening. Susie said, "You go first." I dashed out into the open field toward the house. Suddenly light streaked the sky, and I froze. Then it thundered. A light turned on in Miss Tray's house! Susie screamed, I screamed, and we turned back, running as fast as we could. Was Miss Tray after us?

And then I tripped among the ferns, panicked, out of breath, immobilized. Susie was far ahead. It started to rain. Thunder rumbled, I heard my pounding heart, and I began to cry. But Miss Tray did not come after me. When I finally got up and headed home, the thunderstorm had passed. Crushed pieces of fern were sticking to my clothes and tucked in my hair. Ferns. Whenever I see them now, I remember our game, Miss Tray, and the steamy summer days of my childhood.

Nicki Weiss

31

My parents planted bottles
and flowers in our backyard.
Milk bottles,
Coca-Cola and
root beer bottles,
pickle jars, tall
olive jars, mustard
jars, vinegar jars—
every kind of jar. Among
the bottles, we'd plant
irises and sunflowers
and rhubarb.

Sometimes we'd slip
something inside the
bottles, like dandelion
seeds or tiny books that
we'd made from
pulped newspapers.
And grass would grow
up inside the bottles,
and even ladybugs
would sneak up from below.
People from our community
would all come over
to see our beautiful
walkway, and they'd look
at each other bewildered,
in awe. And we never
took the bottles up, so every
season our bottle garden grew,
making rainbows that glistened
in the midday sun, singing
with the rain and the snow.

Aminah Brenda
Lynn Robinson

Foxglove

When I was a child, my mother had the most beautiful garden. She always grew foxgloves. I would wander through her garden and look for fallen rose pink flowers with purple freckles. I would then place one on each fingertip—my "foxy" gloves. Little did I know that the foxglove is highly poisonous. It is also a valuable medicinal plant that helps thousands of people who have heart problems to lead normal lives. Its seed yields the drug digitalis. My mother took digitalis for fifty years. When I look at foxgloves, I thank them for the years they gave my mother.

Maryjo Koch

When I was young,
during World War II,
families often had victory gardens
in which they grew their own
fruits and vegetables.

Using only a shovel, my father made a victory
garden by digging up our whole backyard. He
dug up the grass we played ball and badminton
on and all the bordering flower beds. It was
exciting, even more exciting when the berry
bushes and vegetables were planted. The garden
grew well: snap peas, radishes, lettuces,
tomatoes, carrots, and my favorite, pole beans,
which grew much taller than I. The harvest was
so good we decided to add to our suburban farm.
We decided to get some chickens.

They arrived at our house in a gunnysack.
My father recklessly opened the sack in our
front hall. Out burst a dozen squawking,
fluttering birds that flew everywhere, even
upstairs into my bedroom. They terrified
me, and I hid in a closet until all of them
had been caught and put into their
new chicken house. To this day
I prefer fruits and vegetables
to chickens.

Gloria Rand

From the age of seven, I wanted
my own apple orchard. I collected seeds
from the tastiest apples, planting them around the yard.
But every two years we moved. I never got to pick an apple.

Later we bought a small farm in the mountains of western Canada.
Outside my window were fifteen apple trees—my dream orchard.
Apple blossoms filled the spring air. In the short, hot summer,
the green fruit soon showed red.

In autumn, as the evenings turned cooler, a mother black bear appeared
with twin cubs. The cubs climbed each tree to shake the apples down.
My precious apples! The bears ate until they were full—a loud crunching—
and kept coming back for more.

One dusky evening, walking out my back door, I almost bumped into the bears.
They looked up, crunching my apples all the while. I knew that bears might
either attack or retreat. They ran. But I ran faster—back into the house.

Thereafter the bears and I made a deal. They gathered apples
every evening. I picked by day. I put the perfect apples in crates
for winter. Bruised apples were made into juice, cider, or pies.
There were enough apples for bears and people.

Erich Hoyt

Amy and I have a big compost pile. All of our *really* good stuff to eat grows from our big compost pile.

One day a watermelon vine grew out of it and crawled up our chain-link fence. Near the top, a watermelon fruit began to grow through the links. Soon the fruit was too fat to push back through and the vine couldn't hold the weight.

So I built a shelf high enough for it to grow on. Each morning I rotated the fruit—nobody wants a flat spot—and it presided there like a king.

David Butler

36

David and I have a big garden. All of the *really* good food we eat comes from our big garden.

I love to grow Kentucky Blue Pole Beans. They cover the stick teepees we build each year. Pablo the cat likes to lie inside the teepees when it gets really hot.

One year the beans grew beyond the teepees and over to our chain-link fence. They would hang and swing in the links. Eventually some beans made it over to Dave's watermelon on the watermelon shelf.

They thought it was the biggest, fattest, laziest pole bean ever.

Amy Butler

Every year I begin my birthday by
going to an old garden where there was
once a farmhouse but now there's only the
garden. All that remains of the garden is a knot of
roses under sumacs that have grown in. When I came to live
here, a neighbor told me about them. She knew I liked roses, and
she knew they were there. What she didn't know is this secret that
only the bees and I know: Every year they start to open on my birthday.

Every year I think it may not happen.

While the light is still new in the morning, I pull on rubber boots to ford the
dew-wet knee-high grass. I take scissors and a jar of water. And I pick roses.
The rose is an old pink rose with a scent you can smell memory in.

Several years ago I dug some roots—thorny sticks—
which I planted in the collection of roses, old irises, and
lavender I call my garden. They've taken now. The same
roses bloom against my stone wall. But still I begin my
birthday going to the old garden. For the ceremony.

A long time ago I learned that we must be the keepers
of our mysteries. The roses are one of mine.

Mary Lyn Ray

38

My wife, Jane, and I moved into our New Hampshire farmhouse twenty-odd years ago. My grandmother, who was born here, had died at ninety-seven and her garden had diminished. The first autumn, Jane planted dozens of daffodils, which flew like goldfinches the following spring. She planted peonies and varieties of lily. Our greatest delight, at the end of our first June, was the outburst of old roses that bloomed near the road: old-fashioned single roses that I remembered from childhood visits to this place and that my mother remembered from her earliest years—red, white, and an outrageous pink. They had endured for a hundred years, surviving drought and hurricane, even salt from Route 4.

Jane gardened all summer, raising prodigious hollyhocks and setting out annuals. We feared that motorists would lose control of their cars, veering in astonishment to see peonies as white as snow and as big as the head of a snowman. But her garden was never quite good enough for Jane. A tulip's unexpected color clashed; moles ate bulbs. Her garden was perfect only in winter, when she stood gazing into borders and hillsides covered with snow, imagining next spring and summer.

After twenty years of grubbing in our dirt, Jane the gardener died, too young, after a long battle with leukemia. I feel too melancholy to take up her flower work. Daffodils thrived this spring, a year after her death, but her peonies shrank to the size of snowballs. Still the old roses endure, nurtured for twenty years by Jane and before her by generations of farm women—blossoms surviving in their frail beauty the long inhabitants of this house, everybody's old roses.

Donald Hall

39

I used to have a pear tree in my backyard.
In winter it caught snowflakes. In spring it
hummed with bees. In summer it hid us from
our enemies. And in autumn, best of all, it gave
us fat, juicy pears—more than we could eat.
So my mother and father canned the excess,
and our family ate pears all year long. I, of course,
got sick of eating pears, and for a long time I did
not eat them. But now, many years later, I can
honestly say that pears are my favorite fruit.

Keith Baker

When I was
young, I planted
sunflower seeds. I
wanted to grow a giant
sunflower as tall as a tree, its
golden head shining down from the blue sky above.
I never could. Every year I planted a seed and waged war
on the slugs in our weedy, sluggy garden, and sometimes
my seedling survived and grew into a tall flower. But I
never grew a giant. I gave up planting sunflower seeds,
believing that truly giant sunflowers were just a myth.

But I was wrong. Last year I saw a real monster
sunflower. It rose up as tall as a tree, its stalk as thick as
a man's thigh, and its golden head shining down from the
sky high above my head.

Now I believe in giants. And this year I'll begin
planting sunflower seeds again.

Christopher Wormell

41

My GRANDFATHER GREW

My grandfather grew
tuberous begonias and everyone
said he had a green thumb.
I would stare at his flowers
and the colors would make
my eyes water: orange, yellow,
pink, scarlet, and white.
I often helped Gramp
in the garden when I visited.
In the winter we would dig up the
bulbs and dust them with white
powder so they wouldn't rot.
We put them in wooden flats
and stored them in the basement.
In spring we put wet peat moss
around each bulb, and when they
sprouted we planted them.

I have a garden of my own now,
and I only wish I had my
grandfather's green thumb.

Karen Barbour

42

flying bulbs

my thumbprint

First snows here are beautiful, but winters are long and white. Even when I'm painting in full color, things look dull. Then it's time for an amaryllis race. I send bulbs to friends around the country, plant my own, and the race begins. Bulbs start sprouting. The stem shoots up rapidly; three, four, five chubby buds appear at the end of the stem, now almost eighteen inches tall. Then boom! The most glorious, colorful flowers open up. One by one friends start calling, describing their blooms, all of us winners. Friendships and flowers grow together on a cold winter's day.

Lois Ehlert

43

Amaryllis

soil line

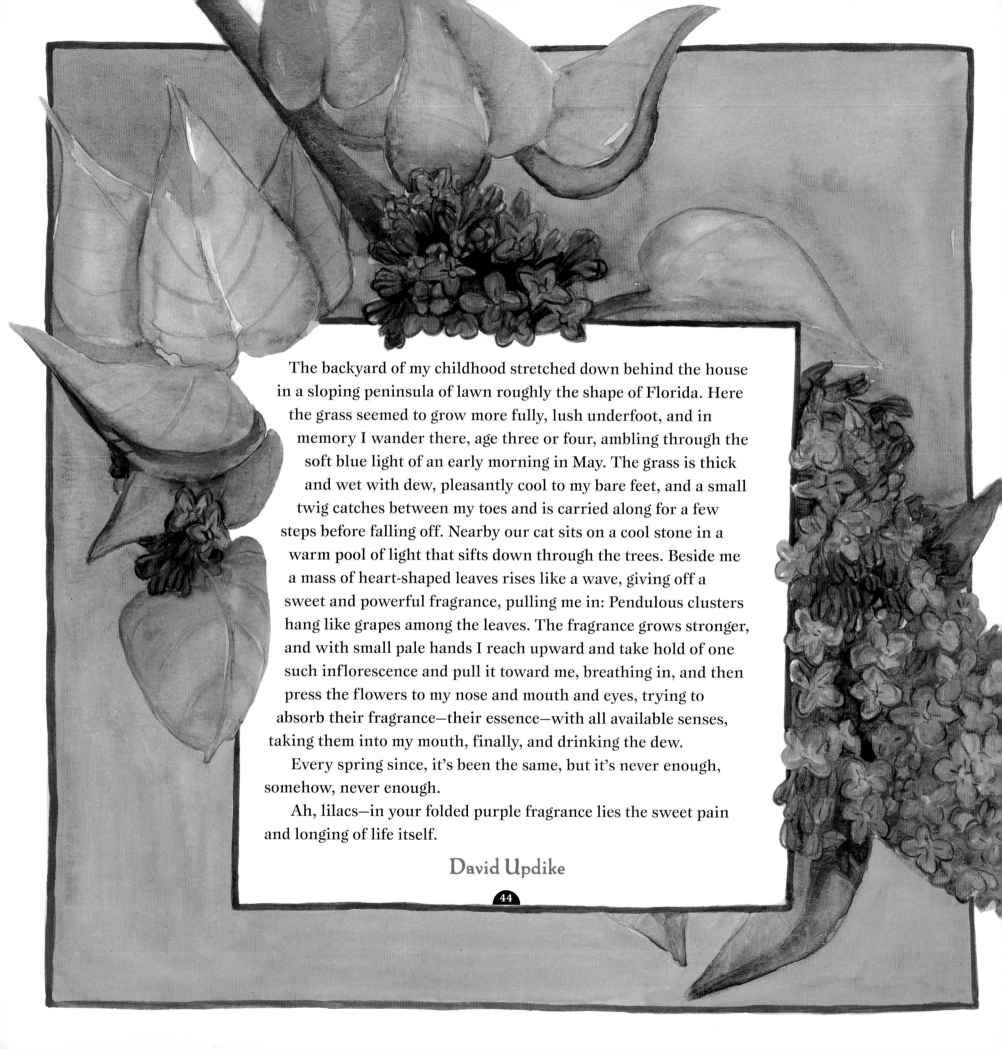

The backyard of my childhood stretched down behind the house in a sloping peninsula of lawn roughly the shape of Florida. Here the grass seemed to grow more fully, lush underfoot, and in memory I wander there, age three or four, ambling through the soft blue light of an early morning in May. The grass is thick and wet with dew, pleasantly cool to my bare feet, and a small twig catches between my toes and is carried along for a few steps before falling off. Nearby our cat sits on a cool stone in a warm pool of light that sifts down through the trees. Beside me a mass of heart-shaped leaves rises like a wave, giving off a sweet and powerful fragrance, pulling me in: Pendulous clusters hang like grapes among the leaves. The fragrance grows stronger, and with small pale hands I reach upward and take hold of one such inflorescence and pull it toward me, breathing in, and then press the flowers to my nose and mouth and eyes, trying to absorb their fragrance—their essence—with all available senses, taking them into my mouth, finally, and drinking the dew.

Every spring since, it's been the same, but it's never enough, somehow, never enough.

Ah, lilacs—in your folded purple fragrance lies the sweet pain and longing of life itself.

David Updike

44

LET'S GET GROWING: ACTIVITIES

SO MANY OF THE STORIES in this collection inspire me to get down to earth—out in my own garden! I wish I could grow flamboyant trees here in Ohio. I wish I had an old pear tree in my yard, a little stream to grow my own willow grove, and old, old roses that my grandparents had planted. But part of gardening is dreaming about gardens, isn't it?

Even if you don't have a garden that can grow everything, you probably have a windowsill, a vase, a kitchen, and a few household items, and that's all that's needed, along with a little patience, to do some of these projects based on the stories you've just read. You can cook up an apple crisp with Jane Ray, make a bean-covered teepee along with Amy Butler, or join in Lois Ehlert's amaryllis race. And that's just for starters.

A few of these projects involve sharp objects, and a few of the recipes require a stove. Always ask an adult's permission or—even better—participation before you begin. Nothing included here is very complicated, expensive, or difficult.

—Michael J. Rosen

KATHI APPELT'S FIGGY FRUIT TREE BELL

Keep the birds from taking all the fruit on your tree by filling the branches with objects that will scare them away with noise and light. Tape pinwheels in the tree. Dangle aluminum pie plates among the branches. And make these tin-can bells with their fishing-weight clappers and cardboard windcatchers.

You will need:

- an empty tin can (remove the wrapper)
- can opener
- a 3-inch round piece of cardboard with a hole punched at the top
- colored markers, paints, or glitter
- 2-1/2–3 feet of string
- a plummet (a fishing weight with an eye)

1. Punch two holes in one end of the can. Remove the other end entirely with a can opener.
2. Use markers, paints, or glitter to color both sides of the cardboard. Waterproof materials work best.
3. Poke the string through the hole in the cardboard. Pull it halfway through and knot it in place.
4. Tie a double knot about two inches from the cardboard. Slip the plummet onto the string and tie another knot.
5. Tie one more double knot, two inches above the weight.
6. Thread each free end of your string up through one of the can's punched holes. Tie them together on the top. Your weight—the bell's clapper—should hang about two inches from the top of the can so it can swing and hit the sides.

Now hang your bell in a fig tree or in any other bird-busy fruit tree.

BOTTLED PEARS

Remember that impossible ship-in-a-bottle trick? You can grow a pear inside a bottle, too.

You will need:

- a narrow-mouthed bottle that can hold a pear inside
- masking tape
- sugar
- a nearby pear tree, of course!

Just wait until a pear tree flowers. Choose a branch on which a fruit has just set—look for a small swelling where a flower has bloomed. Slip a clear, narrow-mouthed bottle over the branch; you may need to remove a few twigs, leaves, and other flowers. Seal the mouth of the bottle with lots of masking tape to keep bugs out and humidity in. Use more tape to hold the heavy bottle on the branch. You might need to prop up the bottle's branch with a stick that has a V-shaped crook at the end.

When the fruit on the rest of the tree has ripened, you'll know that your bottled pear has, too. Untape your bottle and clip the branch close to the mouth of the bottle.

PEAR SYRUP: If you make syrup to fill your bottle, your pear will flavor it. Mix equal parts of sugar and water—two cups of each should do—in a small saucepan and heat the mixture until all the sugar has dissolved. Pour the cooled solution into your bottle, cover it with a cork or a lid, and store your pear in a sunny place. In about a month, you'll have a great pear-flavored syrup that you can use to flavor sodas or to top ice cream, pancakes, and whatever else you enjoy eating with honey or syrup.

You can try this same idea with just-formed grapes.

YOUR OWN FLOWER PRESS

You can create "everlasting" flowers from begonias or most any other flower by making your own flower press from an old phone book.

You will need:

- assorted flowers
- an old phone book or a stack of newspapers
- weights such as books or bricks
- white paper towels

Slip a white paper towel into the book, place a single flower on the center, and cover it with another paper towel (the paper towels help absorb the moisture). Skip a couple dozen pages, and put in your next flower. You can fill the book this way. Once you've finished, put something heavy on top of the closed book, and wait at least two weeks. When you remove the flowers, be extra careful since the petals and leaves will be very brittle.

Once you've dried several kinds of flowers, you can make place mats or bookmarks by pressing your dried specimens between sheets of waxed paper. Arrange your flowers between two sheets of waxed paper. To seal the sheets, ask an adult to warm an iron to a low temperature, then put a thin cloth over and under the waxed paper and iron the two sheets together. You can also add crayon shavings; they'll add other color bursts to the background.

DRYING PRIMROSES AND OTHER FLOWERS

Here are two more ways to dry flowers. Both methods retain most of the flowers' colors and three-dimensional shape. Always pick your flowers early in the day, as soon as the morning dew has evaporated.

1. Gather bunches of flowers, and use a rubber band to hold their ends together. Hang them upside down in a room or shed where there will be some air moving around them. Plants with thorns or with branches that will get especially tangled should be hung individually. Use hooks, nails, clothesline, or similar materials to suspend your flowers. Depending on the temperature of the air and the particular flower, the drying process will take a week or two. Flowers are finished drying when their stalks and flower heads are stiff.
2. You can dry flowers in a box with an inch-thick layer of fine sand. Simply fill a shoe box or other small container with the cleanest, finest sand you can find, place your flowers inside, and then sprinkle more sand over the flowers until they are covered completely. The sand will draw out the moisture in two to four weeks. You can also use clean kitty litter for this job.

   To preserve a branch of leaves, you can soak the branch in a solution made up of water and glycerin—equal parts of both liquids. (Glycerin is an inexpensive syrup available at any drugstore.) First crush the cut end of the branch so that its fibers are exposed, and then place the branch in the solution for two weeks. Glycerin fills the leaves, turning them thicker and sturdier.

AMY BUTLER'S POLE-BEAN TEEPEE

Care to spend a shady summer afternoon inside your own garden teepee? You can make a pole-bean teepee with just three poles and a pack of pole bean seeds! Tomato stakes or any long sticks will work fine. As for the seeds, the Blue Lake is a very old American vine, and the Scarlet Runner Bean is another great choice—its showy red blossoms are a bonus. And, of course, you can harvest beans from your teepee for cooking.

1. Push or hammer three stakes into your garden soil so that they make a stable triangle, with enough room for you to squeeze inside. Fasten their tops together with twine or a heavy rubber band.
2. Sow your seeds according to the packet's directions in a line connecting the three poles. Be sure the soil has warmed up—beans won't germinate in cold weather. If you'd like to have a longer harvesting season, plant half your seeds and leave room among them to add more seeds in a few weeks.
3. Keep your bean teepee watered. You might need to train your vines onto your poles at the beginning. Some gardeners loosely weave string or fishing line between the poles to offer the vines more support.

A HOLLYHOCK HIDEOUT: For a different, more unusual tent, you can plant hollyhocks that will stand six feet tall. No poles necessary! Just plant a packet of seeds a half inch deep, about a foot apart, in a wide circle you can sit inside. (Leave space for a door.) Gather the tops together when the plants reach about five feet tall. Hollyhocks usually resow themselves every year, so you'll always have the start of a new tent—and plenty of company, too: Hollyhocks are favorites of butterflies, bumblebees, and hummingbirds.

A KING-SIZE WATERMELON

The world record for the largest melon is more than 260 pounds! To even come close, experts suggest that you use the Carolina Cross seed, which tends to produce the biggest, though not the tastiest, melons. Here are a few more hints:

- Allow only one or two melons to grow on each plant; more will only divide the plant's giant-producing energy.
- Never grow melons in the same place twice, since they deplete the soil very quickly.
- These big guys really drink up water. (They're not called watermelons for nothing!) Soak their ground at watering times, using warm water if possible.
- And try this: Lightly scratch your name or a message into a melon's skin while it's small. As it grows larger, your letters will also expand. This works with any big member of the squash family (watermelons, cantaloupes, pumpkins, and others).

A DANDY DANDELION SALAD

Small, young dandelion leaves can be picked for an unusual and tangy salad. Gather your greens from a lawn or park that has not been sprayed with fertilizers or chemicals.

- dandelion greens (about one sandwich bag stuffed full)
- one green onion
- one garlic clove
- a tomato (cut in half and squeeze out the seeds)
- chive sprigs
- a strip or two of bacon or soy bacon
- 1/3 cup grated cheese (Swiss or cheddar is fine)
- 1 tablespoon white wine vinegar
- 3 tablespoons olive oil
- ground pepper, pinch of salt

1. Wash, then dry, the dandelion greens very well. Place them in your salad bowl.
2. Chop up the onion, garlic, tomato, and chives, then toss them onto the greens.
3. Fry the bacon in a skillet, and then crumble it on top of your salad. Add the cheese, too.
4. Add the vinegar to the skillet you cooked the bacon in, stir, then add to the salad along with the oil.
5. Add a little salt and pepper until the salad tastes right to you.

If you cover dandelions with inverted flowerpots or small boxes for a week or more before you pick them, the leaves will lose their green color and their taste will be much less bitter. (Did you know dandelions were named by the French, who thought their leaves resembled the "teeth of a lion," in French, *dents-de-lion*?)

A VERY BERRY BIRD WREATH

You can make a wreath that's both beautiful (the birds won't care about that!) and nutritious (that, they'll appreciate). Make, buy, or reuse a wreath of grapevines or evergreen boughs. Then use toothpicks, thread, twist ties, or even rubber bands to hold all sorts of tasty treats in place:

- Gather berries from nearby fields or buy bittersweet berries or pepperberries at a flower shop. You can add sprigs of chokecherries, pyracantha, or holly.
- Use a toothpick to skewer grapes, raisins, dried-fruit bits, or other fruits you may have at home, and fix them to the wreath.
- Tie on pinecones filled with peanut butter and rolled in birdseed.
- String cranberries or popcorn on thread, and wrap around your wreath. (If you make these garlands for your Christmas tree, rehang them on your outside trees and bushes before you dispose of your Christmas tree.)

FIRST AID FOR CUT FLOWERS

Daylilies make beautiful cut flowers. Even though each bloom only lasts a day, a stalk has several buds and they will open on successive days. Whenever you cut flowers, remember to quickly put their cut ends into water. Even a little time without water can cause a plant's water arteries to close. Always use sharp pruning shears or a sharp knife—which means an adult should help with this. If you know you're going out to cut flowers, take along a bucket of water to put the cut stalks in immediately. Here are a few more tips:

- Cut flower stems on an angle, to expose more stem to take in water. After a few days, recut the stems if your flowers are still going strong.
- If your bouquet has turned limp or has been out of water for a bit of time, immerse it entirely—flowers, too—in cold water for a few hours.
- Remove any leaves that will be underwater in your vase.
- Change the water in your vase as soon as it looks cloudy or smells foul.
- Woody stems need to be mashed or split (two inches) to allow for water flow.
- Keep your cut flowers away from warm, sunny windows—in fact, if you have room, store your vase in the refrigerator at night to refresh the flowers.
- Make a fresh flower preservative to help your cut flowers live longer: Mix one crushed aspirin in a solution that is half water and half 7UP.

LOIS EHLERT'S SPRING RAINBOW

In the fall, sometime before the ground freezes, you can plant a spring rainbow. It's always best to ask a gardening friend about the best time for planting in your area and climate. Here's the recipe for one small stretch. Of course, you can continue your rainbow by repeating the pattern as many times as you like.

- *Red:* three Red Emperor tulip bulbs
- *Orange:* three Orange Emperor tulip bulbs
- *Yellow:* three King Alfred daffodil bulbs
- *Blue:* three King of the Blues hyacinth bulbs
- *Green:* all the leaves
- *Purple:* three Early Giant Purple crocus corms

1. Dig up the soil to a depth of 1 foot. Really loosen the soil. You can dig a long trench, an arch shape like a rainbow, or just a circle.
2. Place the bulbs in the trench, 2 inches apart, with their noses up, at the following depths: tulip, 8 inches; daffodil, 7 inches; hyacinth, 5 inches; and crocus, 4 inches.
3. Cover everything with soil and pat down firmly. Water thoroughly. Come spring, even before a rainstorm, you'll find a rainbow spreading across your garden.

DENISE FLEMING'S EASY CHEESY ZUCCHINI

Cheesy zucchini can be a side dish, a filling for an omelette or pita sandwich, or even part of a pasta dish with tomato sauce. It's wonderful cold, too, so you might pack it for lunch on those autumn days when zucchini are overrunning the garden.

You will need:

- about three 8-inch zucchini or one monster zucchini (scoop out the seeds), to give you about 6 cups of grated zucchini
- 1/2 teaspoon salt
- 3 tablespoons butter
- a clove of garlic, chopped very finely
- 2 tablespoons soy sauce
- pepper
- 1/2 cup grated Colby cheese

1. Wash your zucchini and cut off both ends. Coarsely grate them into a colander placed over a bowl or plate to catch juice. Sprinkle with salt and allow the zucchini to stand for twenty-five to thirty minutes.
2. Take handfuls of zucchini and squeeze out the juice. (There will be lots!)
3. Melt butter in a large frying pan. Add minced garlic and sauté for three minutes. Add zucchini, soy sauce, and a dash of pepper to the pan and mix well.
4. Cook this for about four minutes, stirring occasionally. Then turn everything out onto a serving dish and top with grated cheese.

A WINDOWSILL LAWN

It's easy to grow a miniature lawn on your windowsill, and you can use scissors for a lawn mower. Plant your grass in any tray or container that will fit on a windowsill, but be sure you line it completely with heavy plastic so that water won't leak through. Fill your window box with soil about 1-1/2 inches from the top of the container, sprinkle the soil with any grass seeds you have, and then cover the seeds with another inch of soil. Pat down the soil, and water thoroughly but don't flood the seeds. Your seeds should sprout in about a week. If you celebrate Easter at your house with Easter baskets, try this method and use real grass inside your basket. Get started a month or so before Easter to ensure a thick crop in which to nestle your eggs and candies.

A MEMORY GARDEN

Why not plant a friendship garden with bulbs, flowers, and cuttings from all your friends and neighbors—filled with memories of all those fellow gardeners? Label your plants with their scientific or common names and add the names of the people and the places from which they came. Each part of your garden will have a story to tell, a bit of memory that will come back each season along with the plant.

Most gardeners are eager to separate their well-established bulbs, thin their crowded perennials, and gather up the explosions of seedpods, hoping to find new homes for them. Part of the joy in gardening is sharing successes. So why not ask neighbors and friends who share your love of gardening to swap seeds or plants?

Sharing seeds and plants this way also ensures that great old-fashioned plants—many that are sturdier and healthier than newer hybrids—will always be available. Often called heirloom plants, these varieties have unique properties that can be lost with newer hybrids. Your county may have a seed exchange program through which gardeners trade seeds. The Seed Savers Exchange is a national club that operates through the mail. (See the resources section, page 64.) You might like to grow the sort of plants your ancestors grew!

YOUR OWN ORANGERIE, TANGERINERIE, GRAPEFRUITERIE...

Florence Parry Heide's first "garden" was birdseed that germinated in a small jar. You can sprout all kinds of fruits and vegetables with the seeds and pits you'll find around your house, and you don't even need an outdoor garden. You can try lemons, oranges, tangerines, grapefruits, or other citrus plants. Create your own indoor orange grove—an orangerie! But don't count on your trees producing fruit; most trees take years of growing in perfect conditions to become mature enough to blossom and fruit. And don't be disappointed if your seeds just don't sprout—in nature, too, there are always many more seeds than will ever become plants. You might want to start with several of each kind of citrus, to increase the chance of a winner.

Choose the biggest seeds, nick them to remove a tiny part of the hull, and plant each one in a small soil-filled container. Cover the seeds with another half inch of soil. Water your seeds, then cover the container with plastic wrap to hold in the humidity. Keep the soil damp and warm. When the plants sprout, be sure to set them in your sunniest window.

SUNSHINE PICTURE

The sun's rays will print a silhouette of objects that you arrange on paper. You can buy a special photographic paper that sunlight will develop at a hobby or museum shop. It's an inexpensive treated paper that turns from blue to white when it's exposed to sunlight. You can order this paper directly from: Discovery Corner, Lawrence Hall of Science, University of California, Berkeley, CA 94720; (510) 642-1016.

1. Select objects to print. You can make prints of pressed flowers, leaves, or most other flat objects.
2. Place your paper, blue side up, on a piece of cardboard or other flat surface. Do this in a shaded area, and quickly arrange your objects on the paper.
3. Now place the clear acrylic sheet that comes with the paper on top of the objects and take your picture into the sun. Expose it until the blue paper turns white. This could take from one to five minutes. Don't overexpose your picture.
4. Place your print under water for one minute. Then allow it to dry flat.

Some of your finished prints might be suitable for framing; others could become birthday cards or notepaper.

RON HIRSCHI'S WILLOW GROVE

Willow trees are some of the fastest growing of all trees, and their roots are very far-reaching. Home owners should always be careful not to plant a willow close to the house because willow roots can destroy the underground plumbing.

If there is a creek nearby, you can plant willow branches there. Ron suggests that you cut small branches with a sharp knife or pruning shears.

Let the shoots form roots in a jar of water on a windowsill. When you see their new white roots grow to an inch or so, find a spot of soft mud along a stream bank and tuck the newly rooted shoots into their new home. If you're planting more than one, give them plenty of room—ten or twenty feet of space between plants. You'll want to come back often to watch how quickly your new trees take hold…and to see if any moose have moved in.

ERICH HOYT'S APPLE JUICE

By blending different varieties of apples—some sweet and some tart— you can create subtle flavors of apple juice.

You can use a fruit press to extract the juice, but if you don't have one, you can improvise with a juicer or even a meat grinder. If you are picking your own apples, remember: The riper the apple, the more and sweeter juice you will get. Don't worry about bruises. Many apple-juice lovers only use the fallen apples— called windfalls—for making juice. If you are buying apples at a fruit stand or supermarket, you can often find special deals on bruised apples or those with wrinkled skins. Sometimes you can buy a basket of them for almost nothing. They make superb juice.

One secret for juice or cider is to put the apples in the freezer before you press them. If you have a big freezer, put them in a large plastic bag inside it for a few days. Then take the apples out to thaw completely. The pulp will have broken down, making the apples much easier to squeeze.

If you live in a cold climate, try leaving a few of your apples on the trees. In the middle of winter, when the apples are frozen, you can pick them, let them thaw inside, and then easily squeeze out the juice. On a winter's morning it makes a fine, fresh cold juice.

SCUPPERNONG KETCHUP

This recipe is very easy, but it does involve some boiling at the stove, so you'll need an adult to be your assistant chef. If you don't have a good crop of scuppernongs, you can buy Concord grapes. Cook up a batch of this unusual ketchup to try on all the things you usually eat with ketchup.

For each two-cup batch, you will need:

- 2 cups of grapes (remove any stems)
- 1/2 cup water
- 1/2 cup cider vinegar
- 3/4 cup dark brown sugar (packed into the cup)
- 1/2 teaspoon each of ground cloves, ground allspice, ground ginger, and salt
- 1 teaspoon cinnamon
- 1/4 teaspoon freshly ground black pepper

1. Rinse and drain the grapes, and add them to a saucepan with the water. Bring the water to a boil at high heat, then turn it down to simmer for about fifteen minutes until the grape skins have popped and softened.
2. Pour the mixture through a sieve or a fine wire colander into a bowl to remove all the seeds and skins.
3. Return the liquid to the saucepan, add all the other ingredients, and let the mixture simmer again for about thirty minutes or until it has thickened.
4. Turn off the heat, let your ketchup cool, and pour it into clean jars or plastic containers to keep in the refrigerator.

NO-COOK TOMATO SAUCE

There are more recipes for the perfect tomato sauce than you can try in a year, but here's one of the simplest and tastiest—and there's no cooking involved. All you really need is a bumper crop of perfectly ripe tomatoes, and . . .

- 4 tablespoons olive oil
- 1/4 cup chopped basil leaves
- 1/4 cup chopped scallions or shallots
- two cloves garlic, minced (really small pieces)
- some salt and pepper
- some Parmesan cheese to sprinkle on at the end

1. Slice the tomatoes in half, squeeze out the seeds gently, then dice the tomatoes and scoop them into a bowl.
2. Add the first four ingredients to the tomatoes, toss the mixture a bit, and then add salt and pepper until it tastes right to you. Toss it a bit more, and let it sit out, covered, for a few hours. The tomatoes will become much juicier.
3. Prepare whatever kind of pasta you'd like to make for your sauce. Once it's drained, stir the sauce once more and spoon it over the hot pasta, which will warm the sauce. Sprinkle on some cheese, and serve the pasta. (If you planted marigolds with your tomatoes, as Carole King does, you might pluck a couple of blossoms and scatter the top of your pasta with the petals, which are edible!)

PICTURES FROM A MUSHROOM HUNT

Wild mushroom hunting is both an adventure and a science, but because poisonous mushrooms often mimic edible ones, never eat *any* wild mushroom you find.

You can make spore prints with either wild or store-bought mushrooms. This is the method used by mushroom specialists (they're call mycologists) to identify each species of mushroom, since each mushroom has a different kind of spore (the fungus's equivalent of seeds). Your print will be made of the microscopic particles found within the gills (that feathery part) of the mushroom cap.

You will need:

- a piece of white paper
- a glass bowl larger than your mushroom
- any kind of fresh umbrella-type mushroom
- hair spray (optional)

Keep your specimens separate, using small bags or paper cups. Choose only fresh mushrooms. Shriveled or rotting mushrooms have released most of their spores.

1. Remove and discard the mushroom stem. Place the cap in the center of the paper and invert the bowl on top of it.
2. Wait about four hours while the mushroom continues to expand, dropping its spores onto the paper. Carefully lift the bowl to check on your print. If you don't see much progress, leave it for a few more hours or even overnight. (Mushrooms drop their spores at different rates.) The next day carefully lift the bowl, and you'll find the print when you remove your mushroom.
3. To preserve your spore print, spray it quickly with hair spray. Collect your prints in your own mushroom field notebook.

KATHRYN LASKY'S INDOOR MOSS LANDSCAPE

In Maine, where Kathryn lives, moss grows particularly well, but most wooded areas where there's some dampness should offer you many different species of moss. Moss merely clings to the ground, so you can gently lift it free with your fingers. Gather the biggest variety you find, but don't take more than you'll really use.

You will need:

- patches of moss
- a pie tin or shallow dish
- a bit of garden soil
- stones, twigs, and any other miniature landscape material you choose

Fill your container with soil, and "plant" your landscape with pieces of moss. Make hills or valleys by mounding the soil, and add anything else you'd like to your own miniature world: Pebbles become giant boulders; a snippet of a pine frond becomes a tree. What about a pond made from the lens of broken sunglasses? Keep the mosses well watered—mist them with a spray bottle if you can—and they should last all summer and even into the winter. They make interesting centerpieces and great gifts, too. Remember, you can always return the moss to your yard.

GROWING CORN WITH MAXINE KUMIN

Because Maxine lives in New Hampshire, where the growing season is short, she starts her corn in May on a glass-enclosed front porch. Her method guarantees stalks that will be "knee-high by the Fourth of July." Of course, you can't plant your seedlings outdoors until all danger of frost has passed.

You will need:

- a packet of corn seeds
- empty yogurt containers, one for every seed—at least twenty
- a tray, such as an old baking sheet, to hold all your new seed pots
- garden soil

1. Cut the bottoms from each container, then put the lids back on.
2. Prick a hole or two in each lid, turn each container upside down, and fill it with earth. Water the soil thoroughly.
3. Poke a seed about half an inch into the dirt, then cover the whole pot with plastic.
4. Keep your seeds moist by adding water to the tray.

Your seedlings should sprout in a few days. When they're six inches tall, plant them in your garden about fourteen inches apart. When you pop the lids off, the roots may be dangling down; be careful not to break them as you plant them. Corn needs its neighboring corn stalks for company and pollination, so don't try planting corn in one long row. Think of your garden bed as a checkerboard and put your "sproutlings" in each square.

ADAM McCAULEY'S TOPIARY IVY

A topiary is a plant that has been trained into a shape: a simple one, such as a cone or a sphere, or something complicated and even silly, such as a peacock or a bear. Some topiaries are created by constant and selective pruning of the branches until the plants—usually evergreens—attain the desired form. Others are made with chicken wire or another hidden structure on which vines are trained. Some gardeners turn their entire grounds into topiary landscapes.

You can create an easy topiary, either in a pot or in an ivy bed, with a bendable wire coat hanger. Shape the wire (you might need a pair of pliers and/or some adult help) into whatever shape you'd like—a hoop, a jagged tree, a star, or a rabbit—and then insert it gently among the ivy's roots. Carefully twist some of the longer ivy branches onto your wire frame; you might want to twist-tie a branch or two in place at the beginning. As the ivy grows, pinch off any branches that are growing "outside" your shape, or wind them around the vines that are taking the right shape. Topiaries do take time and a little work, so be patient.

MICHAEL McCURDY'S MILKWEED FLEET

During World War II, the fluffy seeds of milkweeds were used as a substitute for kapok (another silky fiber that's obtained from the silk-cotton tree) to create insulation and to fill pillows, mattresses, and life preservers. If there's a bounty of dried milkweed pods, you might be able to gather enough to stuff a small pillow or a pincushion. Or you can always plant a pod of seeds in a sunny patch of soil. You'll start a future home for monarch butterflies, which feast on these amazing plants!

Empty milkweed pods can become small boats for candles. Some warm fall night, convince a couple of adults to have a picnic with you at a pond or a stream. Just before twilight, fix a short birthday candle in the bottom of half a milkweed pod—you can use dripped candle wax, quick-drying glue, or even a bit of chewing gum to hold the candle in place. Once you've assembled your flotilla (that's a fleet of small boats), have the adults light the candles and send the boats out onto the pond. And make some wishes, why not?

POTATO PRINTING WITH DIANA POMEROY

You can print greeting cards, gift wrap, a gardening scarf, or even a frieze for your wall, by cutting and painting a potato. Because carving does involve a knife, be sure you have an adult's participation or permission.

You will need:

- a potato that's firm and large enough to hold
- a sharp knife for whittling
- a rag or washcloth for blotting
- acrylic paints
- some paper or card stock

1. Cut the potato in half, blot the moisture with your rag, and lightly scratch a shape into the cut surface with a pencil.
2. Now use the blade to make a deeper outline of your design.
3. Carve away any part of the potato that isn't a part of your shape, so that your shape stands above the rest of the potato. Blot with your rag as often as needed to remove the moisture. Your design should stand about half an inch above the rest of the potato. If you want to add texture to your design, you can carve shallower lines into the potato.
4. Paint your design. You can use any number of colors you'd like, painting here or there to add shading or pattern. Cover the potato with an even, thick coat of paint.
5. Stamp away! Place your painted potato on your paper, press down evenly and firmly with the palm of your hand, then lift straight up to reveal your first stamp!
6. You can repeat the painting and stamping process as many times as you'd like, using different paints and patterns.

WHAT'S YOUR BIRTHDAY FLOWER?

In addition to having a birthstone, every month also has a flower. Mary Lyn Ray's is the rose, for June. Here's a list so that you can find your official birthday flower.

January: carnation
February: violet
March: jonquil
April: sweet pea
May: lily of the valley
June: rose
July: larkspur
August: gladiola
September: aster
October: calendula
November: chrysanthemum
December: narcissus

Depending on where you live and when you were born, you might be able to plant some of your birthday flowers in your own garden to greet each birthday with you.

JANE RAY'S OWN APPLE CRUMBLE

This warm and crispy dessert will serve five, though it's easy to double the recipe for a bigger crowd.
You will need:

- three or four cooking apples
- 3/4 cup sugar
- pinch of cinnamon
- 1 cup flour
- 5 tablespoons butter or margarine, sliced into bits

1. Grease a 3-inch-deep baking dish with butter. Preheat oven to 400°F.
2. Peel, core, and slice the apples, dropping them in cold water to keep them from turning brown.
3. Drain the apples, and stir in half the sugar and all the cinnamon. Then put the apples into the baking dish.
4. Make the crumble by cutting the butter or margarine into the flour and the remaining sugar until the mixture has the texture of oatmeal. You can use a potato masher or a fork, or you can pinch the mixture together with your fingers.
5. Sprinkle the crumble on top of the apples and bake for twenty minutes.
6. Reduce the heat to 350° F, and continue baking until the crumble is golden and the apple juices are running.

Jane likes to serve this dessert while it's still warm, with a bit of whipped cream on top.

AMINAH BRENDA LYNN ROBINSON'S BOTTLE GARDEN

To create a bottle garden like Aminah's, save any interestingly shaped bottle you find. Bury each one, open end down, in or around your garden among your favorite plants. To make the prettiest garden, choose round and tall vessels, wide- and narrow-mouthed jars, and colored and clear glass.

To grow plants inside the bottles—little individual greenhouses—you'll need to pick clear glass jars or bottles in order for the sunlight to reach the plant; then plant the bottles open side up. Choose plants that won't be too cramped inside or plants that make vines that will creep out of the hole in the top. If your yard is often pounded with rain, you might have to drain your bottles now and then, or keep them protected from flooding.

You will need:

- clear narrow-necked jars
- a piece of stiff paper
- garden soil mixed with some sand
- two long sticks (chopsticks work well)
- a small start of a plant such as ivy

1. Use the stiff paper to make a cone that will fit into the mouths of your bottles and jars. Pour the soil/sand mixture through the cone into the containers.
2. Use the stick to make a hole for your plant, then slide your plant down the cone and into the hole. Remove the cone and use the stick to bury the roots and to scoot soil around the base of the plant.
3. Add a little water, but not too much. Moisture will condense on the glass, adding water to the environment inside. Water only when the soil looks dry.

ROASTED SQUASH SEEDS

Although pumpkin seeds are the most popular for roasting, nearly every variety of squash has large seeds inside that can make a crunchy and nutritious snack.

You will need:

- as many squash seeds as you've got
- a small towel
- a little cooking oil
- a cookie sheet
- salt

1. Lightly oil a cookie sheet and preheat oven to 250°F.
2. Wash the squash seeds, removing all those slimy strings. Pat the seeds dry with a towel, then scatter them in one layer across the cookie sheet.
3. Roast the seeds for thirty minutes, or until they are lightly browned.
4. Stir once during cooking. You'll want an adult's help, of course.
5. Salt the seeds lightly, and let them cool before munching.

JUDY SIERRA'S FRIED MUSTARD GREENS

Mustard greens have an unusual taste since they have the fiery heat of mustard within the red and green leaves. You can try this recipe with other kinds of greens: kale, collard or turnip greens, spinach.

You will need:

- a big bunch of mustard greens
- 1 tablespoon vegetable oil
- 1 teaspoon soy sauce
- 1 tablespoon water
- bacon (or soy bacon) bits (optional)
- maple syrup (optional)

1. Wash the mustard greens, cut off the bottoms of the stems, and then chop them into bite-size pieces.
2. Heat a tablespoon of vegetable oil in a wok or frying pan. Add the mustard and stir for a minute or less, until it's bright green.

3. Turn the heat down low, sprinkle on the soy sauce, add a tablespoon of water, cover, and cook about five minutes. The mustard should be tender but still nice and green. (If you're using thicker, tougher greens, like kale or collards, you might need more cooking time.)

Before serving, Judy often adds some bacon bits or maple syrup, to make the greens extra good.

BRANCHES OF WINTER BLOOMS

Many trees and bushes that are dormant for the colder months can offer up a branch or two for a winter bloom indoors. Lilacs are particularly beautiful and fragrant, but you might also try crab apples, forsythia, pussy willows, and other trees with buds that are set on the branches during the fall.

Choose a small, thin branch from the rear of the plant, so that it won't be missed too much. Use pruning shears or a knife especially suited for cutting wood; you'll want some adult help for this. Pound the bottom half inch of the branch with a hammer so that it splinters, exposing more fibers to absorb water.

Slip the branch in a vase of warm water and place it in a very sunny window. Watch for the buds to open slowly, revealing the flowers just as they would outdoors. Your spring will arrive a little bit earlier, at least on that windowsill.

NICKI WEISS'S FERN PRINTS

You can make beautiful impressions of any fern that you find and even create a field journal to collect your prints.

You will need:

- newspaper to cover your work surface
- a fern frond (or as many kinds as you'd like)
- paints (tempera or acrylic work best)
- blank paper (construction paper, typing paper)
- a brayer or roller

1. Spread out the newspaper and place your fern frond on it. Paint your fern any color or colors that you'd like, trying to coat it evenly and not too heavily.
2. Pick up the frond carefully and set it on clean newspaper, with the ink side up. Then lay a piece of blank paper over the frond, making sure not to move it once you place it down. Now take your brayer and roll it back and forth over the paper. A few times with even pressure will be enough.
3. Lift the paper away from the fern frond slowly to reveal your print. Let it dry, then label it for your field notebook with a caption (what kind it is, where you found it), or decorate it with some special gardening message to give as a gift.

TOWERING SUNFLOWER FEEDERS

The sunflower capital of the United States is Wahpeton, North Dakota, which produces 65 percent of the sunflower crop in this country. Try Mammoth seeds for a very fast-growing plant that will reach twelve feet in three months. (That's an average growth of more than 1-1/2 inches every day!)

If you want to make sunflower feeders for the birds, harvest the heads when they've dropped their petals and store the heads, upside down, in a dry place. Then nail one or two to fence posts or trees around your yard, replacing them with fresh seed heads when the birds have taken most of the seeds.

If you want to eat the seeds yourself, be sure to wait until the seeds are dry and fall out as you rub your hand over the surface of the flower head. Just like the birds, you'll have to remove the black-and-white-striped hull before you eat the seeds. Store the seeds, with or without their hulls, in an airtight container.

A GROWING CONCERN

Share Our Strength and Community Gardens

D URING WORLD WAR II, while soldiers fought overseas, families all across the United States planted victory gardens, converting their backyards into vegetable patches as Gloria Rand's family did (see page 34). Everyone helped: economizing, growing vegetables, rationing foods and resources, and recycling every possible scrap, from old tires to olive pits, from aluminum foil to bacon grease. People everywhere committed themselves to supporting the war effort.

Today there's a different fight being waged, and once again, every member of every community is needed. It's the war on poverty and hunger—not only overseas, not only in countries still wracked by military wars, but in our own neighborhoods. One in every eight children in this country can't be sure that there will be dinner on the table or breakfast before school.

Share Our Strength (SOS), one of the nation's leading antihunger organizations, helps people find ways to end hunger. It has given grants to thousands of school breakfast programs, thousands of community shelters and feeding programs, thousands of agencies aiding people who are homeless, disabled, malnourished, or without families to support them. But, because it takes more than food to fight hunger, SOS has also recruited thousands of chefs and restaurant owners, businesses and corporations, authors and illustrators, to lend their resources and talents.

As odd as it sounds, families in both rural and inner-city neighborhoods in our own country are unable to find or afford fresh fruit and vegetables. To help ease that situation, Share Our Strength has nurtured the community garden, where neighbors choose a site, clear lots, till ground, plant seeds, tend gardens, and finally share in the harvest. Gardeners provide nutritious vegetables and fruits for their own tables, share the harvest with others in the community, or sell their produce at a market to earn money. Each participant in a community garden enjoys the spirit of cooperation, learns gardening and business skills, and helps the community become more beautiful and life supporting.

The success of these small agricultural operations has grown, reaching nearly every city, nearly every poor section of rural America. In Trenton, New Jersey, only three supermarkets served almost 90,000 people, most of whom earned very small incomes. A local community garden program was begun and provided seeds, mulch, compost, and tools, along with lots of advice and expert assistance, to help families transform vacant land into gardens. Now more than 250 gardens and over 2,000 friends and families work these plots, which supply more than $100,000 in fresh produce to the community. Extra produce is sent to local soup kitchens and emergency food centers.

Similar community garden programs offer gardening and nutrition workshops for people who are receiving government assistance, while others have developed popular farmers' markets and produce stands, or work with inner-city immigrants to grow hard-to-find fruits and vegetables that suit their particular diets.

To date, Share Our Strength has granted more than half a million dollars to support more than a hundred community and family gardens and other agricultural projects each year, giving thousands of people access to renewable sources of fresh fruits and vegetables. For instance:

- Kids in Los Angeles grow their own food in a program called From the Ground Up, which not only provides low-income families with fresh produce, but also reclaims the city's vacant lots and trains at-risk kids in leadership and gardening skills.
- Los Niños, located along the border of California and Mexico, teaches mothers and children how to start and maintain a garden in order to provide healthier meals at home.
- The Coalition for a Better Acre in Lowell, Massachusetts, trains Cambodian immigrants to work at intensive vegetable production at a local farm, providing them healthy food and wages.
- SOS supports many gardening projects for native peoples, working to better the health, diet, and well-being of individuals living on and off reservations by affording them a chance to regain their agricultural heritage.

You can be a part of this growing concern by joining with your local antihunger task force or community center, or by contacting one of the organizations listed on page 64. Together we can continue to cast these seeds of commitment and compassion until they have spread and blossomed in hearts everywhere.

—Michael J. Rosen
Columbus, Ohio

For more information about Share Our Strength, other SOS books for children,
or ways that you can become involved in the fight against hunger, write or call:
Share Our Strength, 1511 K Street, Suite 940, Washington, DC 20005; (202) 393-2925.
Or visit the SOS home page on the World Wide Web: www.strength.org

HERE GROWS! SOME SOURCES AND RESOURCES

These organizations and enterprises offer garden supplies, project ideas, starter kits, nature-specific information, and many other materials for the young gardener, teacher, or community group leader.

- National Gardening Association, 180 Flynn Avenue, Burlington, VT 05401; (800) 538-7476. This group has a great newsletter, *Growing Things,* with articles on everything from raising worms to drying herbs. It also has an educational program, GrowLab™, that is a plant-based science laboratory for students of all ages.
- Let's Get Growing, 1900 Commercial Way, Santa Cruz, CA 95065; (800) 408-1868 or (408) 464-1868. This enterprise has a free catalog filled with supplies that pertain to environmental science and nature education. Groups can take advantage of many curricula offered for nature studies. You can also reach Let's Get Growing through its home page on the World Wide Web: http://www.letsgetgrowing.com
- Community Gardens: American Community Gardening Association, 100 North 20th Street, 5th Floor, Philadelphia, PA 19103-1495; (215) 988-8785. These folks are commited to greening projects throughout the United States. The association brings neighbors together to create gardens that improve and beautify neighborhoods while providing food and work for local citizens. If you are a part of a group that would like to join in, be sure to contact this organization.
- The Center for Children's Environmental Literature, P.O. Box 5995, Washington, DC 20016; (202) 237-7301. Founded by children's book author-illustrator Lynne Cherry and supported by the contributions of many concerned authors and illustrators, this nonprofit organization publishes a newsletter for educators that focuses on children's books as a means of appreciating the natural world.
- Operation Green Plant supplies seeds for thousands of community groups throughout the United States that want to beautify natural areas. For information about receiving free seeds for your community group, send a self-addressed, stamped envelope to: Seeds, America the Beautiful Fund, Dept. GD, 1511 K Street, Suite 611, Washington, DC 20005; (202) 638-1649.
- *American Forests Famous & Historic Trees,* 8555 Plummer Road, Jacksonville, FL 32219; (904) 765-0727. This catalog sells trees grown from the seeds of trees at important battlefields, in the yards of renowned Americans, and in other places that are part of our national heritage. You can grow an overcup oak from Abe Lincoln's birthplace, a white ash from Harriet Beecher Stowe's home in Cincinnati, or a bur oak from Mark Twain's favorite boyhood cave. The catalog also features year-long projects such as a "living classroom" and the acorn project, which encourages students to grow a historic oak tree.
- American Horticultural Society, Publications Department, 7931 East Boulevard Drive, Alexandria, VA 22308-1300; (800) 777-7931. All across the United States, gardening groups and botanical societies have special gardens and events tailored for kids and families. The easiest way to find out about such gardens or events near your hometown is to check the society's list of children's gardening programs at public gardens and horticultural societies.
- Native Seeds/SEARCH, 2509 North Campbell Avenue, Suite 325, Tucson, AZ 85719; (520) 327-9123. This organization specializes in seeds grown by native peoples of the Southwest. Write if you are interested in growing early American varieties including giant white sunflowers, Hopi rattle gourds, Navajo blue corn, Mexican ordoño chilies, and even indigo, which makes a blue dye. You can also visit the Native Seeds World Wide Web site: http://Desert.NET/seeds/
- The Seed Savers Exchange, 3076 North Winn Road, Decorah, IA 52101; (319) 382-5990. This nonprofit group is committed to keeping seeds of every variety from becoming extinct. Growers all over the world share their seeds with other gardeners. Exchange members can trade or buy seeds.

No doubt your local garden store or nursery has most of what you could ever want to plant, but there's nothing like a seed catalog, packed with almost endless varieties, to excite (or overexcite) your imagination! Here are two that have plenty of kid-appealing seeds (write or call for free copies).

- Shepherd's Garden Seeds, 30 Irene Street, Torrington, CT 06790; (860) 482-3638. This catalog offers nearly every sort of vegetable from around the world. Or visit the Shepherd's World Wide Web site: http://www.shepherdseeds.com
- Atlee Burpee Company, 300 Park Avenue, Warminster, PA 18974; (800) 888-1447. This is one of the largest and oldest catalogs in the United States.